DO YOU KNOW ME OR JUST THE NAME?

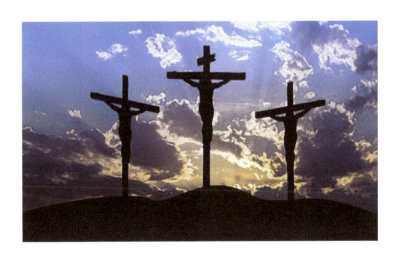

Janet Watson

ISBN 979-8-88943-538-9 (paperback)
ISBN 979-8-88943-539-6 (digital)

Copyright © 2024 by Janet Watson

All rights reserved. No part of this publication may be reproduced, distributed, or transmitted in any form or by any means, including photocopying, recording, or other electronic or mechanical methods without the prior written permission of the publisher. For permission requests, solicit the publisher via the address below.

Christian Faith Publishing
832 Park Avenue
Meadville, PA 16335
www.christianfaithpublishing.com

Printed in the United States of America

Introduction

This book is written to debunk many misconceptions of the Bible. My hope is that you will get his understanding of God and Scriptures that including those who are walking with Christ, who do not know Christ, and those who do not have a relationship with Christ. I pray God will provide you with wisdom and purpose, in any culture and any language all over the world. Amen.

My Story

My name is Janet. My story began when I was a child, about twelve years of age. I was always in church every Sunday with my other siblings, no exception. My mom would leave the house by 4:00 a.m. to go to the wharf where the fishermen were just coming in from fishing. She would purchase different kinds of fish to take back into the town to sell with a small cart on the side of the road, with many other street vendors to make a living to feed us six days a week. Also, on Sundays, she would cook dinner very early and then leave again to see how much she could make that day to pay the bills. My mom had me at a very early age—at fourteen. She didn't finish middle school, and with the help of her mom and dad, she left the countryside to find work in the city. I lived with my grandparents, I believe she said, until her dad died. I was two or three then. My mom was the twelfth child of thirteen children. She returned for me and took me to where she was in the city.

She was not in church, but we had to go to Sunday school and service. I remembered Sunday school more than the service because it was such a long service, about three hours long, as a child, I couldn't wait to go home to eat. I was hungry and sleepy. However, I do remember the preacher (Sister Carmen) always saying "Jesus loves you" to the members. That message stuck with me during my lifetime, and as I grew older, I started to speak to the God whom I didn't know much about but I felt a connection with him. I heard he was in heaven, up in the sky somewhere. I needed to find and talk with him. Life is tough, and I have questions. So this is my story.

My previous church logo was "Know, Grow, and Go for Christ," which makes sense. It is now changed to "Whatever It Takes" to get the Gospel out there.

The question of why we are here and the search for peace is something that resonates with many of us. It's easy to look for peace in the wrong places and people, but we often find that it only adds more stress to our lives. Turning to the book of Genesis to discover why we were created is a powerful reminder that we all have a purpose. We should always be grateful for the support system that we have on our journey towards finding peace and purpose.

I want to give a big shout-out to my previous pastor, teachers, and members of my church family by saying thank you.

The Father, Son, and Holy Spirit: The Trinity

Did you know the Father, Son, Holy Spirit, the heavenly realm, and angels existed before the human race? Let's read Genesis 1 "In the Beginning."

Creation—the heavens:

In the beginning God created the heavens and the earth. The earth was without form, and void; and darkness was on the face of the deep. And the Spirit of God was hovering over the face of the waters.

Then God said, "Let there be light"; and there was light. And God saw the light, that it was good; and God divided the light from the darkness. God called the light Day, and the darkness He called Night. So the evening and the morning were the first day.

Then God said, "Let there be a firmament in the midst of the waters, and let it divide the waters from the waters." Thus God made the firmament, and divided the waters which were under the firmament from the waters which were above the firmament; and it was so. And God called the firmament Heaven. So, the evening and the morning were the second day.

> *Then God said, "Let the waters under the heavens be gathered together into one place, and let the dry land appear"; and it was so. And God called the dry land Earth, and the gathering together of the waters He called Seas. And God saw that it was good. (Genesis 1:1–10)*

Based on what you just read, did God create heaven or heavens?

I'm not sure about you, but I have read this so many times thinking that there was only one heaven, and that was the heavenly realm, where God is. Based on the version of the Bible you are reading, notice that some do say heaven; however, it's heavens. I am currently using the NKJV Bible. *Firmament* definition: "the vault or arch of the sky." That is another heaven.

We now know that he created the heavens. Now let's look at where they are located. The heavenly realm: this is the spiritual realms.

> *For as the rain comes down, and the snow from heaven,*
> *And do not return there,*
> *But water the earth,*
> *And make it bring forth and bud,*
> *That it may give seed to the sower*
> *And bread to the eater,*
> *So shall My word be that goes forth from My mouth;*
> *It shall not return to Me void,*
> *But it shall accomplish what I please,*
> *And it shall prosper in the thing for which I sent it. (Isaiah 55:10–11)*

> *Everything belongs to the Lord your God, not only the earth and everything on it, but also the sky and the highest heavens. (Deuteronomy 10:14)*

DO YOU KNOW ME OR JUST THE NAME?

And take heed, lest you lift your eyes to heaven, and when you see the sun, the moon, and the stars, all the host of heaven, you feel driven to worship them and serve them, which the Lord your God has given to all the peoples under the whole heaven as a heritage. They are not to be worshipped. (Deuteronomy 4:19)

The heavens declare the glory of God; and the firmament shows his handiwork. Who is Jesus Christ? (Psalm 19:1)

Brothers and sisters God is a spirit.

No one has seen God at any time. If we love one another, God abides in us, and His love has been perfected in us. (1 John 4:12)

God is not a man, that He should lie, nor a son of man, that He should repent.
Has He said, and will He not do? Or has He spoken, and will He not make it good? (Numbers 23:19)

As for God, His way is perfect; The word of the Lord is proven; He is a shield to all who trust in him. (2 Samuel 22:31)

Let us read Matthew 1:18–21 and Luke 1:26–28:

Now in the sixth month the angel Gabriel was sent by God to a city of Galilee named Nazareth, to a Virgin betrothed to a man whose name was Joseph, of the house of David. The virgin's name was Mary. And having come in, the angel said to her, "Rejoice, highly favored one, the Lord is with you; blessed are you among women!" (Luke 1:26–28)

This is how the birth of Jesus, the Messiah, came about his mother Mary was pledged to be married to Joseph, but before they came together, she was found to be pregnant through the Holy Spirit. Because Joseph her husband was faithful to the law, and yet did not want to expose her to public disgrace he had in mind to divorce her quietly. But he had considered this, an angel of the Lord appeared to him in a dream, and said "Joseph's son of David, do not be afraid to take Mary home as your wife, because what is conceived in her it's from the Holy Spirit. She will give birth to a son, and you are to give him the name Jesus, because he will save his people from their sins." (Matthew 1:18–21)

The Bible says Jesus was born in Bethlehem that's in Israel born of a virgin. As you can see, he already had made plans to come because he knew that we could not save ourselves from the evil one. This will be discussed later. How many people in your life have ever done or said something like that to you? If they have, you have a true friend.

As Christians, we are to tell everyone about the Gospel of Christ. He came, he died, and he rose again on the third day. That's the Gospel. Jesus came to die (Mark 13:10; Corinthians 9:13).

There are many scriptures in the Bible that talks about Jesus.

Here are some of the Bible scriptures you can read yourself:

1 John 5:7-8—God is more than one person.
1 Peter 1:1-2 – God is more than one person.
Isaiah 7:14—Jesus Christ is God.
Matthew 1:23—God is more than one person.
Ephesians 4:4-6 Everlasting Father
John 1:1–2—God is more than one person.
John 8:58— I Am

DO YOU KNOW ME OR JUST THE NAME?

Exodus 3:14–15—God is more than one person.
John 10:36—Jesus Christ is God.
John 8:24—Jesus Christ is God.
John 14:9-11 —God is more than one person.
2 Corinthians 1:21-22—Jesus Christ is God.
Colossians 1:15–18—God is more than one person.
Philippians 2:5–11—God is more than one person.

The book of John 3:16 talks about the begotten Son; the begotten Son is Jesus, who was there from the beginning. He's considered begotten because he died and was raised again. *Begotten* means in the past, just in case you weren't sure what that means.

> *And the Word was made flesh and dwelt among us, and we behold his glory, as of the only begot-ten son the father, full of grace and truth. (John 1:14)*

God created man and woman:

> *Then God said, "Let Us make man in Our image, according to Our likeness; let them have dominion over the fish of the sea, over the birds of the air, and over the cattle, over all the earth and over, every creeping thing that creeps on the earth." So God created man in His own image; in the image of God He created him; male and female He created them. Then God blessed them, and God said to them, "Be fruitful and multiply; fill the earth and subdue it; have dominion over the fish of the sea, over the birds of the air, and over every living thing that moves on the earth." (Genesis 1:26–28)*

God, man and woman plus child. God considered this to be a family. God does not make mistakes.

Jesus's Ministry

He was a teacher/preacher.
He walked in the footsteps of the Father.
He was not proud.
He only talked about the Father (God).
He did not use eloquent words (persuasive words).
He spoke with authority.
He was a carpenter on earth.

Jesus died and was resurrected. He died at age thirty-three based on Bible verses, and his ministry was three years. Jesus wasn't rich as a human being on earth, and there is nothing wrong with being rich. His ministry was about salvation and all the things that God has to offer, which is life and the kingdom of heaven; one of my favorite verses in *Matthew 6:33*: "*Seek first his kingdom and his righteousness, and all these things will be given to you as well.*" To anyone who trusts, believes, and has faith in him, that is what he taught. Prosperity is inclusive; it is financial and salvation through Christ Jesus.

The Gospel of Jesus Christ

He came, died, and was risen on the third day. Why did Jesus do all this? He did it as a father would do for his children. Sin entered the world with the first humans, Adam and Eve, and from then, everyone sinned. Keep in mind that God knew before time what was to come. (He is eternal Nehemiah 9:5) Yet he still created us. As for me and my house, we do not believe in evolution.

DO YOU KNOW ME OR JUST THE NAME?

Then the Lord saw that the wickedness of man was great in the earth and that every intent of the thoughts of his heart was only evil continually. (Genesis 6:5)

But God demonstrates His love toward us in that while we were still sinners, Christ died for us. Much more than, having now been justified by His blood, we shall be saved from wrath through Him. For if when we were enemies, we were reconciled to God through the death of His Son, much more, having been reconciled, we shall be saved by His life. And not only that, but we also rejoice in God through our Lord Jesus Christ, through whom we have now received the reconcilia- tion. Therefore, just as through one man, sin entered the world, and death through sin, and thus death spread to all men, because all sinned. (Romans 5:8–11)

Therefore, just as through one man sin entered the world, and death through sin, and thus death spread to all men because all sinned—Death in Adam, Life in Christ. (Romans 5:12)

For the Son of Man has come to seek and to save that which was lost. (Luke 19:10)

Just as He chose us in Him before the foundation of the world, that we should be holy and without blame before Him in love. (Ephesians 1:4)

In this is love, not that we loved God, but that He loved us and sent His Son to be the propitiation for our sins. (1 John 4:10)

We are of God. He who knows God hears us; he who is not of God does not hear us. By this, we know the spirit of truth and the spirit of error.

Jesus said to him, "I am the way, the truth, and the life. No one comes to the Father except through Me. If you had known Me, you would have known My Father also; and from now on, you know Him and have seen Him." The father revealed. (John 14:6–7)

Beware lest anyone cheat you through philosophy and empty deceit, according to the tradition of men, according to the basic principles of the world, and not according to Christ. For in Him dwells all the fullness of the Godhead bodily, and you are complete in Him, who is the head of all principality and power. (Colossians 2:8–10)

For the wisdom of this world is foolishness with God. For it is written, "He catches the wise in their own craftiness." (1 Corinthians 3:19)

And the gospel must first be preached to all the nations. (Mark 13:10)

Even so, the Lord has commanded that those who preach the gospel should live from the gospel. (1 Corinthians 9:14)

We are his lost children because of sin. As a parent, is there anything you would not do to help your children? How many times during their lifetime did you say, "Don't do that"? Did they stop because you said stop? I'm sure not all the time. Have you ever felt that you cannot change yourself or others around you? I often find myself saying to the Lord, "You have a big job, and only you can change us." After all, we all have unique personalities that make us who we are.

We cannot change people; God does that, and they must desire to change.

*For we are God's fellow workers; you are God's field;
you are God's building. (1 Corinthians 3:9)*

Do you remember the Burger King ad "Have it your way"? Well, that might be good for Burger King, but not in my house. Nope, you don't get to have it your way. You get to have it your way when you can pay your own bills.

We as parents are not there all the time with our loved ones, but God is. Isn't he awesome? Waiting to forgive us.

His Death

Three times in the Bible, Jesus wept. He was the God-man in the flesh. He knows how we feel and what we go through.

Jesus wept. (John 11:35)

Now as He drew near, He saw the city and wept over it. (Luke 19:41)

Who, in the days of His flesh, when He had offered up prayers and supplications, with vehement cries and tears to Him who was able to save Him from death, and was heard because of His godly fear, though He was a Son, yet He learned obedience by the things which He suffered. And having been per-fected, He became the author of eternal salvation to all who obey Him. (Hebrew 5:7–9)

His Resurrection

His victory over death (Satan).

*He will swallow up death forever,
And the Lord God will wipe away tears from all faces;*

The rebuke of His people
He will take away from all the earth; For the Lord
has spoken.
The Supremacy of God. (Isaiah 25:8)

Psalm 18:1—God the Sovereign Savior

Colossians 1 talks about the supremacy of the Son of God; another great chapter to read.

He is the image of the invisible God, the firstborn over all creation. For by Him all things were created that are in heaven and that are on earth, visible and invisible, whether thrones or dominions or principalities or powers. All things were created through Him and for Him. And He is before all things, and in Him all things consist. And He is the head of the body, the church, who is the beginning, the firstborn from the dead, that in all things He may have the preeminence. (Colossians 1:15–19)

And to make all see what the fellowship of the mystery is, which from the beginning of the ages has been hidden in God who created all things through Jesus Christ. (Ephesians 3:9)

Has in these last days spoken to us by His Son, whom He has appointed heir of all things, through whom also He made the worlds; who being the brightness of His glory and the express image of His person, and upholding all things by the word of His power, when He had by Himself purged our sins, sat down at the right hand of the Majesty on high. (Hebrews 1:2–3)

As you can see, after he died for our sins, where is he sitting? On the right hand of God, the Father. Do you know that he intercedes (pray for us) to the father? Because he came and lived as a man, he understands what we go through.

Let's look at the comparison of Jesus to God the Father

He is the Messiah.

He loves righteously; that is his nature.

He is the radiance and exact representation of God nature.

He walks with the Father God.

He does nothing without the Father.

He is God anointed.

He is a high priest.

He does not change, just like the Father. He has all the qualities of the Father.

He is the Savior of the world.

He reigns forever. His throne is in the heavenly realm

He is the Alpha and the Omega, which means the beginning and the end, the first and the last.

God's Son is greater than the angels.

Jesus was raised from the dead, the only God-man that was raised from the dead.

He is the radiance of God's glory.

He made purification for our sins.

He sat down at the right hand of God in the heavenly realm.

Jesus is heir to all things.

Below are some of the ways God speak to us:

God is not a feeling, so it must not be based on feeling it must be based on his word. With prayer and dedication, you will hear his voice; it's unique, and again, it takes time for you to recognize it.

1. God speaks through the church, the people.
2. God speaks through the Bible, his Word.
3. God speaks through the Holy Spirit, who is now in us as Christians.
4. God speaks through circumstances and trials.

5. God speaks through prayer. Let's practicing listening more and speaking less. This is how you get to know his voice. Don't be deceived, there are many voices in this world.

There are many other ways God had spoken before; all through the Bible, God's directions are specific. If you read the Old Testament, you will see when he gives Moses, David, Elijah, Abraham, and other directions, everything is specific on how he would like it done. The entire book of the Bible is good reading. God also repeats himself more than once in the chapters. When you must say to someone the same thing repeatedly, isn't it to say to that person, I am serious about this?

God's Nature

God is love.

> *For God so loved the world that He gave His only begotten Son, that whoever believes in Him should not perish but have everlasting life. (John 3:16)*

> *And now abide faith, hope, love, these three; but the greatest of these is love. (1 Corinthians 13:13)*

> *He who does not love does not know God, for God is love. (1 John 4:8)*

God's Attributes

God is knowing (omnipresent)—he is present all the time (Romans 11:33–34; 2 Chronicles 16:9).
God is omnipotent—he is all-powerful; he has unlimited power and authority (Psalm 62:11).
God is immutable—he is unchangeable (Numbers 23:19).
God is sovereign—he superior to all others, in control of everything, and does everything (Isaiah 46:9–10).

DO YOU KNOW ME OR JUST THE NAME?

God is faithful—he is loyal and dependable (Deuteronomy 7:9).
God is holy—he is perfect (Exodus 15:11).
God is just—he is righteous (2 Chronicles 19:7).
God has a standard (Ezekiel 16).
God is wise—he judges rightly (Proverbs 2:6).
God is eternal—he existed before time and is everlasting (Nehemiah 9:5b).
God is supreme—he is superior (Job 11:7–9)
God is the Creator—he created the universe and life (Genesis 1:1).
God is good—he is upright (Psalm 119:68).

These are some of the names of God:

Immanuel: God with us
Jehovah Robi: the Lord is my shepherd
Elohim: the all-powerful Creator
Jehovah: the self-revealing one
Adonai: the owner of all
Jehovah-Jireh: the Lord who provides
El Shaddai: the almighty sufficient one
El Eliot: the most high ruler
Jehovah Nissi: the Lord's banner of victory
Jehovah Shalom: the Lord our peace
Jehovah Mekadesh: the Lord who sanctifies
Jehovah Rophe: the Lord who heals
Jehovah Tsikenu: the Lord my righteousness
Which one of the above names resonate with you?

What Are the Fruits of the Spirit?

> But the fruit of the Spirit is love, joy, peace, kindness, goodness, faithfulness, gentleness, self-control. Against such there is no law. (Galatians 5:22–23)

What are your fruits of the spirit?

Why Are We Here?

*Everyone who is called by My name, Whom I have
created for My glory.
I have formed him, yes, I have made him. (Isaiah
43:7)*

*I will praise You; I am fearfully and wonderfully
made; Marvelous are Your works, And that my soul
knows very well. (Psalms 139:14)*

Now I was asked this question a few times in my ministry, and just like you, I had wondered about it as well. This was when I first started in ministry, so I enrolled in a deeper understanding in Bible classes. I had prayed, asking the Lord what I needed to do to have a closer walk with him. I'm sure you have asked yourself this question as well.

*For we are His workmanship, created in Christ Jesus
for good works, which God prepared beforehand
that we should walk in them. (Ephesians 2:10)*

We are here to have a relationship with Christ Jesus. He created us to have a love relationship with him. You are wonderfully made. You have a purpose for being here. You are not your own; you were bought with a price.

*For you were bought at a price; therefore, glorify
God in your body and in your spirit, which are
God's. The blood he shed on the cross for us sinners.
(1 Corinthians 6:20)*

If you want to have a relationship with Jesus Christ, you must make yourself available and give the Holy Spirit total control of you so he can change you. I read once that I cannot stay in the same mindset that I am in now to walk with God, and I have to want this as well. Many newborn Christians, just as when I was starting out, thought that by believing and baptizing, they would change overnight, and all their problems would be behind them. No, it will not; this is a process.

We must learn to persevere through all tribulations in life. We're not going to learn everything overnight, and we're not going to change overnight; but that does not mean he's not working even though you don't see it. Continue to make yourself available, be committed, endure, and open-minded to learn. Have you ever been hungry for his word? I have.

> *That no one should be shaken by these afflictions; for you yourselves know that we are appointed to this. (1 Thessalonians 3:3)*

Affliction is great suffering.

> *No temptation has overtaken you except as is common to man; but God is faithful, who will not allow you to be tempted beyond what you are able, but with the temptation will also make the way of escape, that you may be able to bear it. (1 Corinthians 10:13)*

Did you know that as a Christian, you have a special angel watching over you? It's true! And have you ever had an experience where something happened, but you missed it or were too caught up in the moment to notice? I know I have.

Or someone swiped you off the road, but God took care of it by taking hold of the steering wheel? I usually say thank you, Lord. Angels are messengers of the Lord. How do you typically thank him?

> *No one can come to Me unless the Father who sent Me draws him, and I will raise him up on the last day. (John 6:44)*

No one can come to Christ unless the Father draws him. Are you being drawn to him but refusing him? What is the reason? Have you experienced conviction or guilt when you don't do what you are asked to do? I have.

As Christians, we are sanctified; this means "set apart."

And you belong to Christ; and Christ belongs to God. (1 Corinthians 3:23)

As Christians we must decrease for God to increase:

He must increase, but I must decrease. (John 3:30)

Jesus answered, "Most assuredly, I say to you, unless one is born of water and the Spirit, he cannot enter the kingdom of God. That which is born of the flesh is flesh, and that which is born of the Spirit is spirit. Do not marvel that I said to you, 'You must be born again.'" (John 3:5–7)

This is baptism.

Who Are We Fighting?

For we do not wrestle against flesh and blood, but against principalities, against powers, against the rulers of the darkness of this age, against spiritual hosts of wickedness in the heavenly places. (Ephesians 6:12)

Blessed is the man who endures temptation; for when he has been approved, he will receive the crown of life which the Lord has promised to those who love Him. (James 1:12)

DO YOU KNOW ME OR JUST THE NAME?

Spiritual Battles, Warfare

Lucifer/the devil/ Satan/prince of darkness—the morning star:

*You were the anointed cherub who covers; I estab-
lished you;
You were on the holy mountain of God;
You walked back and forth in the midst of fiery
stones. (Ezekiel 18:14)*

*When the morning stars sang together,
And all the sons of God shouted for joy? (Job 38:7)*

*How you are fallen from heaven,
O Lucifer, son of the morning!
How you are cut down to the ground,
You who weakened the nations!
For you have said in your heart:
"I will ascend into heaven,
I will exalt my throne above the stars of God. I will
also sit on the mount of the congregation On
the farthest sides of the north.
I will ascend above the heights of the clouds, I will
be like the Most High."
Yet you shall be brought down to Sheol,
To the lowest depths of the Pit. (Isaiah 14:12–15)*

*So, the great dragon was cast out, that serpent of old,
called the Devil and Satan, who deceives the whole
world; he was cast to the earth, and his angels were
cast out with him. (Revelation 12:9)*

Why was Lucifer cast out of heaven? He desired to take the place of God and have power over the Creator. Interestingly, he was the music leader in heaven. It is said that some of the music we listen to influences events happening in the world. Hence, it is crucial to consider what children are exposed to in terms of music and media consumption."

Lucifer does not possess the same powers as God. He is described as the father of lies, crafty, and the ruler of this world.

> *We know that we are of God, and the the whole world lies under the sway of the wicked one. (1 John 5:19)*

As Christians, we need to ask God for discernment.

How to Fight: Armor of God

> *For we do not have a High Priest who cannot sympathize with our weaknesses, but was in all points tempted as we are, yet without sin. (Hebrews 4:15)*

> *For we do not wrestle against flesh and blood, but against principalities, against powers, against the rulers of the darkness of this age, against spiritual hosts of wickedness in the heavenly places. Therefore take up the whole armor of God, that you may be able to withstand in the evil day, and having done all, to stand. (Ephesians 6:12–13)*

> *Stand therefore, having girded your waist with truth, having put on the breastplate of righteousness, and having shod your feet with the preparation of the gospel of peace; above all, taking the Shield of faith with which, you will be able to quench all the fiery darts of the wicked one. And take the helmet of salvation, and the sword of the Spirit, which is the word of God; praying always with all prayer and supplication in the Spirit, being watchful to*

DO YOU KNOW ME OR JUST THE NAME?

this end with all perseverance and supplication for all the saints—and for me, that utterance may be given to me, that I may open my mouth boldly to make known the mystery of the gospel. (Ephesians 6:14–19)

For the weapons of our warfare are not carnal but mighty in God for pulling down strongholds, casting down arguments and every high thing that exalts itself against the knowledge of God, bringing every thought into captivity to the obedience of Christ. (2 Corinthians 10:4–5)

By the word of truth, by the power of God, by the armor of righteousness on the right hand and on the left. (2 Corinthians 6:7)

For the message of the cross is foolishness to those who are perishing, but to us who are being saved it is the power of God. (1 Corinthians 1:18)

What Is Prayer?

Prayer is access to God and is a two-way conversation. The model prayer: "Our father who art in heaven." Do you know that *Matthew 6:5–15* is an example of how to pray? Not a prayer to constantly repeat, that is like drinking milk. This is considered going to church to listen to the pastor for a few hours but never read the Bible.

> *Anyone who lives on milk, being still an infant, is not acquainted with the teaching about righteousness. (Hebrews 5:13)*

Have you been reading the Word of God, or are you complacent with just going to church on Sundays or one day a week? When you pray, do you end your prayer with "Thy will be done in Christ Jesus," or do you say amen? Both are important. Many of us tend to talk more and listen less. With that said, how are you going to hear the voice of God when he responds?

Do you value prayer time? There are twenty-four hours in a day, which equals to 1,440 minutes within a day and 10,800 minutes in a week. How many of that is spent on talking to your Creator? God will not force anyone to come to him.

> *Now this is the confidence that we have in Him, that if we ask anything according to His will, He hears us. And if we know that He hears us, whatever we ask, we know that we have the petitions that we have asked of Him. (1 John 5:14–15)*

The New Testament gave an example of how to pray. This is how we should pray; we begin with *Luke 11:1–11; Matthew 6:5–13*:

Our Father—worship him.
Praise him—for all the things he has done.
Forgiveness of others—forgive others so you will be forgiven.
Request—make your request
Worship—close with worship and "Your will be done," not my mind.

Look at how prayer was done in some of the chapters. Daniel 2:19–23 and Jeremiah 32:16–25, and their prayers were answered.
They prayed with an earnest heart.

Galatians 6:2 says, "*Carry each other's burdens, and in this way you will fulfill the law of Christ.*"

The Hypercritical Prayer

But let him ask in faith, with no doubt, for he who doubts is like a wave of the sea driven and tossed by the wind. For let not that man suppose that he will receive anything from the Lord. (James 1:6–7)

The sacrifice of the wicked is an abomination to the Lord, But the prayer of the upright is His delight. (Proverbs 15:8)

We know that God does not listen to sinners. He listens to the godly person who does his will. (John 9:31)

How Many Years Is One Day to God?

It is said that one thousand years is considered one day to God. As a child, I was always told that God is coming, and I kept looking for him, but he never came. Think for a minute if it takes one thousand years for one day, and we are in 2022, how many days is it to God?

> *But, beloved, do not forget this one thing, that with the Lord one day is as a thousand years, and a thousand years as one day. (2 Peter 3:8)*

What Does God Require of Us?

Obedience—God wants us to make wise decisions. We gain knowledge, but God is the one that gives us wisdom; no one or anywhere else. God sees the motives of our hearts, not the exterior features.

> *Therefore, if anyone is in Christ, he is a new creation; old things have passed away; behold, all things have become new. (2 Corinthians 5:17)*

> *But when the Pharisees heard that He had silenced the Sadducees, they gathered. Then one of them, a lawyer, asked Him a question, testing Him, and saying, "Teacher, which is the great commandment in the law?"*
> *Jesus said to him, "'You shall love the Lord your God with all your heart, with all your soul, and with all your mind.' This is the first and great commandment. And the second is like it: 'You shall love your neighbor as yourself.' On these two commandments hang all the Law and the Prophets." (Matthew 22:34–40)*

> *But I say to you, love your enemies, bless those who curse you, do good to those who hate you, and pray for those who spitefully use you and persecute you. (Matthew 5:44)*

DO YOU KNOW ME OR JUST THE NAME?

Pursue peace with all people, and holiness, without which no one will see the Lord. (Hebrews 12:14)

But He gives more grace. Therefore, He says: "God resists the proud, But give grace to the humble."

Therefore, submit to God. Resist the devil and he will flee from you. Draw near to God and He will draw near to you. Cleanse your hands, you sinners; and purify your hearts, you double-minded. Lament and mourn and weep! Let your laughter be turned to mourning and your joy to gloom. Humble your-selves in the sight of the Lord, and He will lift you up. (James 4:6–10)

Where Is God?

He is everywhere. God is omnipresent.
The Lord looks down from heaven upon the chil-dren of men,
To see if there are any who understand, who seek God. (Psalm 14:2)

Till the Lord from heaven
Looks down and sees. (Lamentations 3:50)

The eyes of the Lord are on the righteous, And His ears are open to their cry.
The face of the Lord is against those who do evil,
To cut off the remembrance of them from the earth.
The righteous cry out, and the Lord hears,
And delivers them out of all their troubles. (Psalm 34:15–17)

Who Is the Bible Created For? Everyone

The Bible is created for everyone. Have you tried reading the Bible by yourself and didn't understand a word of it? I have. In order to fully know what the Bible is saying, the Holy Spirit will give you the knowledge and wisdom you need, as well as bring people in your life to assist you when you have questions.

> *Not by works of righteousness which we have done, but according to His mercy He saved us, through the washing of regeneration and renewing of the Holy Spirit. (Titus 3:5)*

> *But know that the Lord has set apart for Himself him who is godly. The Lord will hear when I call to Him. (Psalms 4:3)*

Who Are Christians?

Christians are believers and followers of Christ Jesus.

> *For it is by grace you have been saved, through faith, and this is not from yourselves, it is the gift of God, not of works so no one can boast, for we are God's handiwork, created in Christ to do good works, which God prepared in advance for us to do. (Ephesians 2:8–10)*

> *And have put on the new man, which is renewed in knowledge after the image of him that that created him. (Colossians 3:10)*

> *But the Helper, the Holy Spirit, whom the Father will send in My name, He will teach you all things, and bring to your remembrance all things that I said to you. Peace I leave with you, My peace I give*

DO YOU KNOW ME OR JUST THE NAME?

to you; not as the world gives do I give to you. Let not your heart be troubled, neither let it be afraid. (John 14:26–27)

Buried with Him in baptism, in which you also were raised with Him through faith in the working of God, who raised Him from the dead. And you, being dead in your trespasses and the uncircumcision of your flesh, He has made alive together with Him, having forgiven you all trespasses, having wiped out the handwriting of requirements that was against us, which was contrary to us. And He has taken it out of the way, having nailed it to the cross." (Colossians 2:12–14)

As far as the east is from the west, so far has He removed our transgressions from us. (Psalms 103:12)

All unrighteousness is sin, and there is sin not leading to death. (1 John 5:17)

Therefore, do not let sin reign in your mortal body, that you should obey it in its lusts. (Romans 6:12)

Do you not know that your bodies are members of Christ? Shall I then take the members of Christ and make them members of a harlot? Certainly not! Or do you not know that he who is joined to a harlot is one body with her? For "the two," He says, "shall become one flesh." But he who is joined to the Lord is one spirit with Him.

    Flee sexual immorality. Every sin that a man does is outside the body, but he who commits sexual immorality sins against his own body. Or do you not know that your body is the temple of the Holy Spirit who is in you, whom you have from God, and you are not your own? (1 Corinthians 6:15–19)

Christ's Resurrection/His Return: The Great Commission

Then the eleven disciples went away into Galilee, to the mountain which Jesus had appointed for them. When they saw Him, they worshiped Him; but some doubted.

And Jesus came and spoke to them, saying, "All authority has been given to Me in heaven and on earth. Go therefore and make disciples of all the nations, baptizing them in the name of the Father and of the Son and of the Holy Spirit, teaching them to observe all things that I have commanded you; and lo, I am with you always, even to the end of the age." Amen. (Matthew 28:16–20)

But I do not want you to be ignorant, brethren, concerning those who have fallen asleep, lest you sorrow as others who have no hope. For if we believe that Jesus died and rose again, even so God will bring with Him those who sleep in Jesus. (1 Thessalonian 4:13–14)

Our spiritual body:

It is sown a natural body; it is raised a spiritual body. There is a natural body, and there is a spiritual body. (1 Corinthians 15:44)

Now this I say, brethren, that flesh and blood cannot inherit the kingdom of God; nor does corruption inherit incorruption. (1 Corinthians 15:50)

God's Favorite

God has no favorite. God does not look at the color of your skin. We are all created by him. We are all important to him. We are all God's children. We all have the same-color blood—it's red. Once again, we are wonderfully made, even the ones that has a disability. It's okay to love them; they are people too. Help them, care for them, and tell them they are beautiful. Nothing in life is easy; that's what my momma said. God bless her soul.

For there is no partiality with God. *(Romans 2:11)*

Tithes and Offerings

Will a man rob God?
Yet you have robbed Me!
But you say,
"In what way have we robbed You?" In tithes and
offerings. You are cursed with a curse,
For you have robbed Me,
Even this whole nation.
Bring all the tithes into the storehouse,
That there may be food in My house,
And try Me now in this,
Says the Lord of hosts,
"If I will not open for you the windows of heaven
And pour out for you such blessing
That there will not be room enough to receive it."
(Malachi 3:8–10)

You shall truly tithe all the increase of your grain that
the field produces year by year. (Deuteronomy
14:22)

I fast twice a week; I give tithes of all that I possess.
(Luke 18:12)

I have heard people say God doesn't need money. This is true however, all through the Bible, God talks about giving tithes and offerings. The first tithe was given by Abraham to Melchizedek, the first high priest in Genesis. In those days, it was crops, animals, etc. One-tenth of what you earn. Together we can make a difference in our communities by supporting our churches. They cannot operate on their own. These days it's donations and volunteering. There are brothers and sisters and pastors who work in the offices, etc., to continue God's ministry. If they misuse the funds for personal reasons, God will deal with it.

> *Therefore judge nothing before the time, until the Lord comes, who will both bring to light the hidden things of darkness and reveal the counsels of the hearts. Then each one's praise will come from God. Good or bad what is hidden in darkness will come to light but be aware of surroundings. There are ways to deal with unrighteous people. (1 Corinthians 4:5)*

Growing in Christ

To grow in Christ requires obedience and endurance through experience. That's how you get to know Christ. Once again, it is not a feeling. In the book of John, after Jesus had risen, he said, "We have a great high priest, that is passed into the heavens, Jesus the Son of God, let us hold fast our profession."

> *Therefore, since we have a great high priest who has ascended into heaven, Jesus the Son of God, let us hold firmly to the faith we profess. (Hebrews 4:14)*
>
> *Let all bitterness, wrath, anger, clamor, and evil speaking be put away from you, with all malice. (Ephesians 4:31)*

DO YOU KNOW ME OR JUST THE NAME?

John 15:5 states, *"I am the vine, ye are the branches: He that abideth in me, and I in him, the same bringeth forth much fruit, for without me ye can do nothing."*

Ephesians 5:18 says, *"Be not drunk with wine, wherein is excess; but be filled with the spirit."*

> *Let heaven and earth praise him, the seas, and everything that moves in them. (Psalms 69:34)*

> *He who sins is of the devil, for the devil has sinned from the beginning. For this purpose, the Son of God was manifested that He might destroy the works of the devil. (1 John 3:8)*

What Is Faith?

Faith is confidence in what you hope for and assurance about what we do not see (Hebrew 11:1).

Jesus went on to say, "If you have faith as small as a mustard seed you can say to the Mountain, move and it will move." (Matthew 17:20)

Here are some additional verses you can look up: *Matthew 21:21; James 2:17.*

You can't just say it and do nothing about it. Someone once told me God won't move until you move. Asking and not seeking to find it will not work. Praying and sitting, waiting for it—it depends on the situation. You must do your part. Remember the verse, *"So I say to you, ask, and it will be given to you; seek, and you will find; knock, and it wll be opened to you" Luke 11:9.*

Many people believe that all you must do is ask for it, and it will be delivered to you—not all the time, but the Bible says if it is God's will. We all feel disappointed, and sometimes we end up expressing our frustration to those around us; this should never be. There is a reason for everything. God knows best so it was not something he believed was best for you. When we do ask, and we receive it (ask, knock, and seek), then we glorify ourselves as though we did it on our own. No, you didn't. Make sure to glorify God, not yourself. We cannot do it on our own.

Walking by Faith

Faith comes from hearing the message. Faith by itself, if it is not accompanied by action, is dead.

> *For we walk by faith, not by sight. (2 Corinthians 5:7)*

> *He who is faithful in what is least is faithful also in much; and he who is unjust in what is least is unjust also in much. (Luke 16:10)*

> *And without faith it is impossible to please God. (Hebrews 11:6)*

> *Romans 13:14 "But put he on the Lord Jesus Christ and make not provision for the flesh to fulfill the lust thereof."*

> *But know that the Lord has set apart him that is godly for himself the Lord will hear when I call onto him. (Psalms 4:3)*

This is not an easy task, but it can be done; I am an example.

Spiritual Gifts

For I say, through the grace given to me, to everyone who is among you, not to think of himself more highly than he ought to think, but to think soberly, as God has dealt to each one a measure of faith. For as we have many members in one body, but all the members do not have the same function, so we, being many, are one body in Christ, and individually members of one another. Having then gifts differing according to the grace that is given to us, let us use them: if prophecy, let us prophecy in proportion to our faith; or ministry, let us use it in our ministering; he who teaches, in teaching; he who exhorts, in exhortation; he who gives, with liberality; he who leads, with diligence; he who shows mercy, with cheerfulness. (Romans 12:3–8)

There are diversities of gifts, but the same Spirit. There are differences of ministries, but the same Lord. And there are diversities of activities, but it is the same God who works all in all. But the manifestation of the Spirit is given to each one for the profit of all: for to one is given the word of wisdom through the Spirit, to another the word of knowledge through the same Spirit, to another faith by the same Spirit, to another gift of healings by the same Spirit, to another the working of miracles, to another prophecy, to another discerning of spirits,

DO YOU KNOW ME OR JUST THE NAME?

to another different kinds of tongues, to another the interpretation of tongues. But one and the same Spirit works all these things, distributing to each one individually as He wills. (1 Corinthians 12:4–11)

And He Himself gave some to be apostles, some prophets, some evangelists, and some pastors and teachers, for the equipping of the saints for the work of ministry, for the edifying of the body of Christ, till we all come to the unity of the faith and of the knowledge of the Son of God, to a perfect man, to the measure of the stature of the fullness of Christ. (Ephesians 4:11–13)

As each one has received a gift, minister it to one another as good stewards of the manifold grace of God. If anyone speaks, let him speak as the oracles of God. If anyone ministers, let him do it as with the ability which God supplies, that in all things God may be glorified through Jesus Christ, to whom belong the glory and the dominion forever and ever. (1 Peter 4:10–11)

What Is the Main Issue with Humans?

Disobedience

Here are the things we do - We grieve the Holy Spirit.

And do not grieve the Holy Spirit of God, by whom you were sealed for the day of redemption. (Ephesians 4:30)

We tend to talk more and listen less.
We do not like authority.
We complain all the time.

We tend to worship idols (idols are objects, people, or things that take the place of God) (Deuteronomy 6:15).
Overall, we tend to forget God's goodness and mercies.

We are selfish people. We tend to:

Have no compassion for one another
Be prideful
We glorify ourselves
Murder others that we did not create
Lie and steal from each other
Disregard other cultures as insignificant

Where do wars and fights come from among you? Do they not come from your desires for pleasure that war in your members? (James 4:1)

Some strongholds:
Pride (Proverbs 18:12, 24:16; Jeremiah 13:15)
Stress
Preoccupation
Priorities (Ephesians 5:15; Proverbs 3:5–6)
    Living for the world and other people (1 John 2:15–17)

*There are six things the Lord hates,
seven that are detestable to him:
haughty eyes,
a lying tongue,
hands that shed innocent blood,
a heart that devises wicked schemes,
feet that are quick to rush into evil,
a false witness who pours out lies*

DO YOU KNOW ME OR JUST THE NAME?

and a person who stirs up conflict in the community.
(Proverbs 6:16–19)

The wicked, in his proud countenance, does not seek
God.
God is in none of his thoughts. (Psalms 10:4)

Let's look at scriptures: Hebrews 7:22; Deuteronomy 28:1–8 and 15–20, Romans 8:7; 1 John 5:4, 2:16; 1 Corinthians 5:9-10.

For we know Him who said, "Vengeance is Mine,
I will repay," says the Lord. And again, "The Lord
will judge His people. (Hebrews 10:30)

We suffer because of sin.

The Bible considers sin as death, not physical death but separation from God. God is light. God is life. If you continue to be separated from God when you physically die, then there is no repentance of sin. It is too late.

I have been to a few funerals in my lifetime and have seen people praying to God for the souls of the dead. Can you really pray for the soul of the dead or pray for God to comfort the family and friends of the dead?

We sin because of the prince of darkness who comes to kill, steal, and destroy. He tempts you to sin. The first human that sinned was Adam and Eve. In the book of Genesis, it states that God told Adam not to eat of a specific tree in the garden of Eden, but he can eat of all everything else. However, Eve was tempted by the snake (Lucifer), the devil, the prince of darkness, whatever name you may use (Genesis 1:26–28).

The Narrow and the Wide Gate

Enter by the narrow gate; for wide is the gate and broad is the way that leads to destruction, and there are many who go in by it. Because narrow is the gate and difficulty is the way which leads to life, and there are few who find it. (Matthew 7:13–14)

Do not love the world or the things in the world. If anyone loves the world, the love of the Father is not in him. For all that is in the world—the lust of the flesh, the lust of the eyes, and the pride of life—is not of the Father but is of the world. And the world is passing away, and the lust of it; but he who does the will of God abides forever. (1 John 2:15–17)

Therefore do not let sin reign in your mortal body so that you obey its evil desires. (Roman 6:12)

Lucifer—Ephesians 4:26-27; James 4:7; 1 Peter 5:9; Isaiah 14:12

Which gate are you choosing?

Satan Thrown Out of Heaven

And war broke out in heaven: Michael and his angels fought with the dragon; and the dragon and his angels fought, but they did not prevail, nor was a place found for them in heaven any longer. So the great dragon was cast out, that serpent of old, called the Devil and Satan, who deceives the whole world; he was cast to the earth, and his angels were cast out with him. (Revelation 12:7–9)

And no wonder! For Satan himself transforms himself into an angel of light. (2 Corinthians 11:14)

DO YOU KNOW ME OR JUST THE NAME?

In which you once walked according to the course of this world, according to the prince of the power of the air, the spirit who now works in the sons of disobedience. (Ephesians 2:2)

Prepare your hearts.

But seek first the kingdom of God and His righteousness, and all these things shall be added to you. (Matthew 6:33)

Do you have any idea how someone can get to know God?

Repentance—a change of heart

Know Christ. Grow in Christ. Go for Christ

As it is written: "There is none righteous, no, not one" (Romans 3:10).

For all have sinned and fallen short of the glory of God. (Romans 3:23)

But your iniquities have separated you from your God; And your sins have hidden His face from you So that He will not hear. (Isaiah 59:2)

For the wages of sin is death, but the gift of God is eternal life in Christ Jesus our Lord. (Romans 6:23)

For God so loved the world that He gave His only begotten Son, that whoever believes in Him should not perish but have everlasting life. (John 3:16)

And saying, "The time is fulfilled, and the kingdom of God is at hand. Repent, and believe in the gospel." (Mark 1:15)

I have not come to call the righteous, but sinners, to repentance. (Luke 5:32)

I say to you that likewise, there will be more joy in heaven over one sinner who repents than over ninety-nine just persons who need no repentance. (Luke 15:7)

Likewise, I say to you, there is joy in the presence of the angels of God over one sinner who repents. (Luke 15:10)

God's Instructions

The Ten Commandments uphold the law.

And God spoke all these words, saying:

"I am the Lord your God, who brought you out of the land of Egypt, out of the house of bondage.

"You shall have no other gods before Me.

"You shall not make for yourself a carved image— any likeness of anything that is in heaven above, or that is in the earth beneath, or that is in the water under the earth; you shall not bow down to them nor serve them. For I, the Lord your God, am a jealous God, visiting the iniquity of the fathers upon the children to the third and fourth generations of those who hate Me, but showing mercy to thousands, to those who love Me and keep My commandments.

"You shall not take the name of the Lord your God in vain, for the Lord will not hold him guiltless who takes His name in vain.

"Remember the Sabbath day, to keep it holy. Six days you shall labor and do all your work, but the seventh day is the Sabbath of the Lord your God. In it you shall do no work: you, nor your son, nor your daughter, nor your male servant, nor your female servant, nor your cattle, nor your stranger who is within your gates. For in six days the Lord made the heavens and the earth, the sea,

and all That is in them and rested the seventh day. Therefore, the Lord blessed the Sabbath day and hallowed it.

"Honor your father and your mother, that your days may be long upon the land which the Lord your God is giving you.

"You shall not murder.

"You shall not commit adultery.

"You shall not steal.

"You shall not bear false witness against your neighbor.

"You shall not covet your neighbor's house; you shall not covet your neighbor's wife, nor his male servant, nor his female servant, nor his ox, nor his donkey, nor anything that is your neighbor's." (Exodus 20)

I am the Lord, that is My name;
And My glory I will not give to another,
Nor My praise to carved images. (Isaiah 42:8)

Leviticus 18, 20; 1 Corinthians 5:10-11

Do not judge, or you too will be judged. (Matthew 7:1)

Trust in the Lord with all your heart, And lean not on your own understanding. (Proverbs 3:5)

For those who live according to the flesh set their minds on the things of the flesh, but those who live according to the Spirit, the things of the Spirit. (Romans 8:5)

Because the carnal mind is enmity against God; for it is not subject to the law of God, nor indeed can

DO YOU KNOW ME OR JUST THE NAME?

be. So then, those who are in the flesh cannot please God. (Romans 8:7–8)

Keep in mind, the Ten Commandments will not save you. Grace is what saves you. The Ten Commandments were given to show us what we are doing wrong. The law condemns us.

Things we must do:

Therefore, as the elect of God, holy and beloved, put on tender mercies, kindness, humility, meekness, long suffering; bearing with one another, and forgiving one another, if anyone has a complaint against another; even as Christ forgave you, so you also must do. But above all these things put on love, which is the bond of perfection. And let the peace of God rule in your hearts, to which also you were called in one body: and be thankful. Let the word of Christ dwell in you richly in all wisdom, teaching and admonishing one another in psalms and hymns and spiritual songs, singing with grace in your hearts to the Lord. And whatever you do in word or deed, do all in the name of the Lord Jesus, giving thanks to God the Father through Him. (Romans 3:12–17)

But your iniquities have separated you from your God; And your sins have hidden His face from you so that He will not hear (Deuteronomy 6:13)

Things we must not do:

If then you were raised with Christ, seek those things which are above, where Christ is, sitting at the right hand of God. Set your mind on things above, not on things on the earth. For you died, and your life is hidden with Christ in God. When Christ

Who is our life, appears, then you also will appear with Him in glory.

Therefore put to death your members which are on the earth: fornication, uncleanness, passion, evil desire, and covetousness, which is idolatry. Because of these things the wrath of God is coming upon the sons of disobedience, in which you yourselves once walked when you lived in them.

But now you yourselves are to put off all these: anger, wrath, malice, blasphemy, filthy language out of your mouth. Do not lie to one another, since you have put off the old man with his deeds, and have put on the new man who is renewed in knowledge according to the image of Him who created him, where there is neither Greek nor Jew, circumcised nor uncircumcised, barbarian, Scythian, slave nor free, but Christ is all and in all. (Colossians 3:1–11)

Flee sexual immorality. Every sin that a man does is outside the body, but he who commits sexual immorality sins against his own body. Or do you not know that your body is the temple of the Holy Spirit who is in you, whom you have from God, and you are not your own? For you were bought at a price; therefore, glorify God in your body and in your spirit, which are God. (1 Corinthians 6:18–20)

You shall not curse the deaf, nor put a stumbling block before the blind, but shall fear your God: I am the Lord. (Leviticus 19:14)

DO YOU KNOW ME OR JUST THE NAME?

Give no regard to mediums and familiar spirits; do not seek after them, to be defiled by them: I am the Lord your God. (Leviticus 19:31)

Therefore you shall not oppress one another, but you shall fear your God; for I am the Lord your God. (Leviticus 25:17)

The Christian Home

Wives, submit to your own husbands, as is fitting in the Lord.

Husbands, love your wives and do not be bitter toward them.

Children obey your parents in all things, for this is well pleasing to the Lord.

Fathers, do not provoke their children, lest they become discouraged.

Bondservants, obey in all things your masters according to the flesh, not with eye service, as men-pleasers, but in the sincerity of heart, fearing God. And whatever you do, do it heartily, as to the Lord and not to men, knowing that from the Lord you will receive the reward of the inheritance; for you serve the Lord Christ. But he who does wrong will be repaid for what he has done, and there is no partiality. (Colossians 3:18–25)

Fathers shall not be put to death for their children, nor shall children be put to death for their fathers; a person shall be put to death for his own sin. (Deuteronomy 24:16)

Other Bible verses you can read. The term "submit" is sometimes misinterpreted or misused by women. It is generally associated with the act of yielding to the will or authority of someone else. However, in some cases, women may use the word "submit" to imply a sense of subservience or inferiority.

This can be problematic as it reinforces gender stereotypes and can lead to unequal power dynamics in personal and professional relationships. It is important to understand the true meaning of the word "submit" and to use it appropriately in context. Please remember that God created man to be the provider and the protector of the family and the woman as his helper. I know in these times it may not be exactly what is happening now. Raise the child in a godly manner with the wisdom of God, not of the world.

> *Train up a child in the way he should go, and when he is old, he will not depart from it. (Proverbs 22:6)*
>
> *Chasten your son while there is hope, And do not set your heart on his destruction. (Proverbs 19:18)*
>
> *Correct your son, and he will give you rest; Yes, he will give delight to your soul. (Proverbs 29:17)*
>
> *But if anyone does not provide for his own, and especially for those of his household, he has denied the faith and is worse than an unbeliever. (1 Timothy 5:8)*
>
> *I say then: Walk in the Spirit, and you shall not fulfill the lust of the flesh. For the flesh lusts against the Spirit, and the Spirit against the flesh; and these are contrary to one another, so that you do not do the things that you wish. But if you are led by the Spirit, you are not under the law. (Galatians 5:16–18)*

Leviticus 18, 20:10–23
Matthew 18:15–20

Test Yourself

Romans 8:37—We are more than conquerors.
James 1:21—Doers, not hearers only.

Therefore lay aside all filthiness and overflow of wickedness, and receive with meekness the implanted word, which is able to save your souls.

That the genuineness of your faith, being much more precious than gold that perishes, though it is tested by fire, may be found to praise, honor, and glory at the revelation of Jesus Christ. (1 Peter 1:7)

For I say, through the grace given to me, to everyone who is among you, not to think of himself more highly than he ought to think, but to think soberly, as God has dealt to each one a measure of faith. (Romans 12:3–3)

The Imperative of Love

In this the children of God and the children of the devil are manifest: Whoever does not practice righteousness is not of God, nor is he who does not love his brother. (1 John 3:10)

Examine yourselves as to whether you are in the faith. Test yourselves. Do you not know yourselves, that Jesus Christ is in you?—unless indeed you are disqualified. (2 Corinthians 13:5)

The book of Proverbs tells you how to live. Great reading as well.

DO YOU KNOW ME OR JUST THE NAME?

The Parable of the Sower:

And again, He began to teach by the sea. And a great multitude was gathered to Him, so that He got into a boat and sat in it on the sea; and the whole multitude was on the land facing the sea.

Then He taught them many things by parables and said to them in His teaching: "Listen! Behold, a Sower went out to sow. And it happened, as he sowed, that some seed fell by the wayside; and the birds of the air came and devoured it. Some fell on stony ground, where it did not have much earth; and immediately it sprang up because it had no depth of earth. But when the sun was up it was scorched, and because it had no root it withered away. And some seed fell among thorns; and the thorns grew up and choked it, and it yielded no crop. But other seeds fell on good ground and yielded a crop that sprang up, increased, and produced: some thirtyfold, some sixty, and some a hundred." And He said to them, "He who has ears to hear, let him hear!"

But when He was alone, those around Him with the twelve asked Him about the parable. And He said to them, "To you it has been given to know the mystery of the kingdom of God; but to those who are outside, all things come in parables, so that 'Seeing they may see and not perceive, And hearing they may hear and not understand;

Lest they should turn,

And their sins be forgiven them

And He said to them, "Do you not understand this parable? How then will you understand all the parables? The Sower sows the word. And these are the ones by the wayside where the word is sown. When they hear, Satan comes immediately and takes away the word that was sown in their hearts. These like-

wise are the ones sown on stony ground who, when they hear the word, immediately receive it with gladness; and they have no root in themselves, and so endure only for a time. Afterward, when tribulation or persecution arises for the word's sake, immediately they stumble. Now these are the ones sown among thorns; they are the ones who hear the word, and the cares of this world, the deceitfulness of riches, and the desires for other things entering in choke the word, and it becomes unfruitful. But these are the ones sown on good ground, those who hear the word, accept it, and bear fruit: some thirtyfold, some sixty, and some a hundred." (Mark 4:1–20)

Which one are you?

God's Promises

*Even to your old age, I am He,
And even to gray hairs, I will carry you!
I have made, and I will bear.
I will carry and will deliver you. (Isaiah 46:4)*

Through the Lord's mercies we are not consumed, Because His compassions fail not. They are new every morning; Great is Your faithfulness. (Lamentations 3:22–23)

Other verses: 1 John 3:1; John 16:23; Matthew 21:22; Luke 11:9; John 15:7

Revelation: Coming of Christ, Judgment

Reading the book of Revelation in a group setting can be a powerful experience. It's easy to feel sad when we read about people who choose not to follow the path, we believe is right. However, it's

DO YOU KNOW ME OR JUST THE NAME?

important to keep in mind that this can also be an opportunity for reflection and growth. By going deeper into the text, we can find inspiration in the reasons why some choose to follow Christ. Let's keep an open heart and mind as we continue to explore this powerful book together.

As Christians, it's important to remember that our actions speak louder than our words. We must strive to live a life that reflects our faith and values and be obedient to God's will in all things. While others may not always see the hidden motives and agendas of those around us, we can take comfort in knowing that God sees the true nature of our hearts. Let us be true to ourselves and our beliefs and remember that we are called to a higher standard.

Think on this for a minute: if you are upright and trying your best to walk right, or if you don't care for people who lie or steal, would you offer that person a room in your home knowing that this person constantly does these things? What happens if you have kids? Do you fear they will see and imitate them? I would not, so why would a righteous God allow you to live in his kingdom? We all will be judged (Galatians 6:7). One bad apple infects the entire bunch.

> So it will be at the end of the age. The angels will come forth, separate the wicked from among the just. *(Matthew 13:49)*

> For the Son of Man will come in the glory of His Father with His angels, and then He will reward each according to his works. *(Proverbs 16:27)*

> But no one knows of that day and hour, not even the angels of heaven, but My Father only. *(Proverbs 24:36)*

Other verses: Revelations 21:4, 7:9, 12:10, 22:3-4; Psalm 27:4; Ecclesiastes 12:14 -it is finished.

The Fear of God

I once spoke to a new believer who was hungry for Christ Jesus. I thought, *This is great.* While we talking, I stated that our problem is disobedience, and he will judge us, and he gets angry based on many chapters in the Old Testament. She was shocked.

You see, just like most of us, we only know the love of God, and we believe that God loves us. He never gets angry. Yes, he does. Here are some chapters in the Old Testament where God got angry and destroyed many people when they questioned his decisions. We do ask many things, don't we? I have always thanked God for Jesus because he is sitting on the right hand of God, interceding for us.

> *They have turned away backward:*
> *Alas, sinful nation,*
> *A people laden with iniquity,*
> *A brood of evildoers,*
> *Children who are corrupters!*
> *They have forsaken the Lord,*
> *They have provoked anger*
> *The Holy One of Israel,*
> *They have turned away backward. (Isaiah 1:4)*

> *He cast on them the fierceness of His anger, Wrath,*
> *indignation, and trouble.*
> *By sending angels of destruction among them.*
> *(Psalm 78:49)*

> *For we know Him who said, "Vengeance is Mine,*
> *I will repay," says the Lord. And again, "The Lord*
> *will judge His people." It is a fearful thing to fall into*
> *the hands of the living God. (Hebrews 10:30–31)*

Heavenly realm (*Deuteronomy 10:14*)

The Rapture

Now this I say, brethren, that flesh and blood cannot inherit the kingdom of God; nor does corruption inherit incorruption. Behold, I tell you a mystery: We shall not all sleep, but we shall all be changed—in a moment, in the twinkling of an eye at the last trumpet. For the trumpet will sound, and the dead will be raised incorruptible, and we shall be changed. For this corruptible must put on incorruption, and this mortal must put on immortality. So when this corruptible has put on incorruption, and this mortal has put on immorality, then shall be brought to pass the saying that is written: "Death is swallowed up in victory.

"O Death, where is your sting? "O Hades, where is your victory?"

The sting of death is sin, and the strength of sin is the law. But thanks be to God, who gives us the victory through our Lord Jesus Christ.

Therefore, my beloved brethren, be steadfast, immovable, always abounding in the work of the Lord, knowing that your labor is not in vain in the Lord. (1 Corinthian 15:50–58)

But I do not want you to be ignorant, brethren, concerning those who have fallen asleep, lest you sorrow as others who have no hope. For if we believe that Jesus died and rose again, even so God will bring with Him those who sleep in Jesus.

For this we say to you by the word of the Lord, that we who are alive and remain until the coming of the Lord will by no means precede those who are asleep. For the Lord Himself will descend from heaven with a shout, with the voice of an archangel, and with the trumpet of God. And the dead in

Christ will rise first. Then we who are alive and remain shall be caught up together with them in the clouds to meet the Lord in the air. And thus, we shall always be with the Lord. Therefore comfort one another with these words. (Thessalonians 4:13–18)

So, we are always confident, knowing that while we are at home in the body, we are absent from the Lord. For we walk by faith, not by sight. We are confident, yes, well pleased rather to be absent from the body and to be present with the Lord. (2 Corinthians 5:6–8)

As you can see based on the above passage, we will have a new body when we are caught up to meet him. The word *Hades* above is hell.

In Heaven

Indeed heaven and the highest heavens belong to the Lord your God, also the earth with all that is in it. (Deuteronomy 10:14)

There is no sin. (1 Corinthians 6:9-10)
There are no tears. (Revelation 7:17)
We will see and be with the Lord.
No curse (Revelation 22:3-5; Psalm 103:19, 115:3).
No more pain or suffering. (Revelation 21:1-4)
No marriage in heaven (Matthew 22:30).
No death. (Revelation 21:4)

Righteousness and justice are the foundation of Your throne; Mercy and truth go before Your face. (Psalm 89:14)

DO YOU KNOW ME OR JUST THE NAME?

Many who miss the kingdom of God:

They follow the crowd (Matthew 7:13).
They have no hope.
They do not believe.
They have no faith.
They don't like authority.
They refuse instructions.
Their heart is hardened.

Few Who Enter the Kingdom of God: Revelation

The narrow way:

> *And He went through the cities and villages, teaching, and journeying toward Jerusalem. Then one said to Him, "Lord, are there few who are saved?"*
>
> *And He said to them, "Strive to enter through the narrow gate, for many, I say to you, will seek to enter and will not be able. When once the Master of the house has risen up and shut the door, and you begin to stand outside and knock at the door, saying, 'Lord, Lord, open for us,' and He will answer and say to you, 'I do not know you, where you are from,' then you will begin to say, 'We ate and drank in Your presence, and You taught in our streets.' But He will say, 'I tell you I do not know you, where you are from. Depart from Me, all you workers of iniquity.' There will be weeping and gnashing of teeth when you see Abraham and Isaac and Jacob and all the prophets in the kingdom of God, and yourselves thrust out. They will come from the east and the west, from the north and the south, and sit down in the kingdom of God. And indeed, there are the last who will be first, and there are first who will be last." (Luke 13:22–30)*

Come to Me, all you who labor and are heavy laden, and I will give you rest. Take My yoke upon you and learn from Me, for I am [a]gentle and lowly in heart, and you will find rest for your souls. (Matthew 11:28–29)

Most assuredly, I say to you, he who hears My word and believes in Him who sent Me has everlasting life, and shall not come into judgment, but has passed from death into life. (John 5:24)

In My Father's house are many mansions; if it were not so, I would have told you. I am going to prepare a place for you. And if I go and prepare a place for you, I will come again and receive you to Myself; that where I am, there you may be also. (John 14:2–3)

They had faith—they believe, they walk with Jesus Christ, they are obedient, they walked the narrow way instead of the wide way (the world way).

Reward: salvation, life, ruler in heaven with Christ Jesus.

Run to Win

Therefore, do not worry about tomorrow, for tomorrow will worry about its own things. Sufficient for the day is its own trouble. (Matthew 6:34)

Again, the kingdom of heaven is like a merchant seeking beautiful pearls. (Matthew 13:45)

Let your conduct be without covetousness; be content with such things as you have. For He Himself has said, "I will never leave you nor forsake you." (Hebrews 13:5)

DO YOU KNOW ME OR JUST THE NAME?

Be content, be always grateful. Praise and worship no matter what your circumstances are. Practice this daily. So run to win, be in control of your actions, and persevere. Christians read God's love letters to you.

Romans 12:9–21—behave like Christians.

Conclusions

2 Corinthians 9:8; Hebrews 4:12

Do you have an urgency to follow God? For the younger generations, if you have a mother and grandmother or anyone that needs your assistance in reading the Bible, please take a few minutes and download an app for them so they can listen to the Scriptures, as there are Bible apps that do read the Scriptures. It would really be a big help to them with just a few minutes from you.

To everyone who shares the Gospel of Jesus Christ, like Paul says, "I am not ashamed of the Gospel. (Romans 1:16)" Do not be ashamed; you will have oppositions, so do this: *"And whoever will not receive you nor hear your words, when you depart from that house or city, shake off the dust from your feet" (Matthew 10:14)*. Pray and move on. There is always someone else out there that wants to hear the Gospel. Do not get discouraged; do not get upset and angry. The word *no* is not a bad word. We sometimes tend to see it as fighting words, but it is not. Also, do not look at it as they are rejecting you (*1 Samuel 8:7*). Jesus Christ says they are rejecting him. So, it's okay. Pray for them and let go and let God. Keep in mind that you cannot change people; God does that.

In this world, we live once, so do your best. Here is a saying I always remember. I don't know who wrote this, but here it is: "I passed this way but once, whatever I can do for you let me do it now as I will never pass this way again. You may have heard it as well or something like it. Be blessed."

When you are lost, he will find you.

What man of you, having a hundred sheep, if he loses one of them, does not leave the ninety-nine in the wilderness and go after the one which is lost until he finds it? (Luke 15:4)

I, even I, am He who blots out your transgressions for My own sake;
And I will not remember your sins. (Isaiah 43:25)

These things I have spoken to you, that in Me you may have peace. In the world, you will have trib-ulation, but be of good cheer; I have overcome the world. (John 16:33)

Brothers and sisters, it is finished. The devil has no power over you. Jesus paid the price for your sins; your sins are forgiven. Take up your cross, believe and persevere.

Be Encouraged

Here is one of my favorite poems. It's called "I Am There." During one of the darkest times in my life, I came upon this poem, and it meant a lot to me. I replaced it with "I Am Here." You can do this.

Do you need me? I am there.
You cannot see me, yet I am the light you see
    by You cannot hear me, yet I speak through
    your voice
You cannot feel me, yet I am the power at work
    in your hands.
I am at work, thought you do not understand
    my ways

DO YOU KNOW ME OR JUST THE NAME?

I do not have strange visions. I am not mysteries
    Only in absolute stillness, beyond self, can
    you
know me as I am,
and then but as a feeling and a faith
Yet I am there, yet I hear. Yet I answer.
When you need me, I am there
Even if you deny me, I am there
Even when you feel most alone, I am there
Even in your fears, I am there
Even in your pain, I am there
I am there when you pray and when you do not
    pray
I am in you, and you are in Me
Only in your mind can you feel separate from
    me, For only
In your mind are the mists of "yours" and "mine".
    Yet only with your mind can you know me
    and experience me
Empty your heart of empty fears
When you get yourself out of the way, I am there
You can of yourself do nothing, but I can do all
And I am in all
Though you may not see the good, good is there,
    for I am there
I am there because I have to be, because I am Only in Me
    does the world have meaning; only.
Out of Me does the world take form.
only because of Me does the world go forward
I am the law on which the movement of the stars
and the growth of living cells are founded.
I am the love that is the laws fulfilling.
I am assurance
I am peace.
I am oneness.

I am the law that you can live by I am the love
   that you can cling to I am your assurance I
   am your peace
I am one with you.
I am
Though you fail to find me, I do not fail you
   Though your faith in Me is unsure, My
   faith in you never waivers,
Because I know you, because I love you.
Beloved, I am there.
(By Astronaut James B. Irwin)

Ephesians 6:10
Romans 15:13
Romans 1:11–16
1 Corinthians 2:5
Colossians 1:3
2 Corinthians 12:9
1 John 2:5
Psalms 95:7
Psalm 100:3
Philippians 4:4
1 Samuel 12:24

Fear

2 Timothy 1:7
Proverbs 10:20
Proverbs 15:2
Luke 21:26

*For as many as are led by the Spirit of God, these
are sons of God. For you did not receive the spirit of
bondage again to fear, but you received the Spirit of
adoption by whom we cry out, "Abba, Father." The
Spirit Himself bears witness with our spirit that we*

DO YOU KNOW ME OR JUST THE NAME?

are children of God, and if children, then heirs—
heirs of God and joint heirs with Christ, if indeed
we suffer with Him, that we may also be glorified
together. (Romans 8:14–17)

God must be first-Matthew 10:37-39 False prophets—Matthew 24:24 Holy Spirit—John 1:14; Acts 2:32
God is judge—Acts 4:12, 17:26–28
Revelation 20:11–13; Ezekiel 18:4
Perish—1 Timothy 6:16
Revelation 21:7-8
Baptism—Acts 2:38; Isaiah 5:30
You must be born again—John 3:3, 5–6;
1 Corinthians 15:50–54
Begotten—1 Peter 1:3–4; Hebrews 2:11; Matthew 12:50 Angels—Psalm 29:1; Hebrews 1:14
Immorality—1 Corinthians 5:10–11; Matthew 7:1 Blasphemy—Matthew 12:30–32
Idols—anything that is man-made and takes the place of God Freedom in Christ—1 Corinthians 10:23, 6:12; heaven or hell, life
or death (separation for God)
Forgiveness—Matthew 18:21, 25:41, 46; Revelation 20:11–15 Trials—James 1:2–8; 2 Corinthians 13:9; Romans 8:28–30 Warnings—Isaiah 5:20; Matthew 18:6; Luke 18:15-17
Psalm 9:1
Marriage—Genesis 2:24; Hebrews 13:4–6
Separation from God (death)—Romans 1:18–28, 2
Sin—Romans 7
Government—Romans 13:1–7
Fools—Ecclesiastics 10:3
Riches—Jeremiah 9:23
Money—1 Timothy 6:10, 17
Spiritual immaturity—Hebrews 5:12–14
Christ's death—Hebrews 10:5–7
Heavenly voice—Hebrews 12:25

Grace—Ephesians 2:5–8
Peace—John 14:27
Redeem—1 Peter 1:11–19
The comforter—John 14:21, 1:26
A place for you—John 14:2–3
Love each other—John 13:34
Rewards—Romans 14:10; 1 Samuel 26:23; 2 Chronicles 15:7; Matthew 5:12; Luke 6:23

It is finished John 19:30

Grace by Kay Arthur
G-God's R-Riches A-At C-Christ's E-Expense.
(Kay Arthur)

For if we have been united together in the likeness of His death, certainly we also shall be in the likeness of His resurrection. (Roman 6:5)

T-Thank G-God I-for his F-Faithfulness
L-Love O-Others V-Value E-Each other.

Praise and Worship

"Wide as the Sky," Isabel Davis, https://music.youtube.com/watch?v=075R8XfybJM&list=RDAMVMcyzbge2QEF4.

"No Greater Love," Rudy Clarence and Chrisette Michele, https://music.youtube.com/watch?v=-3vjDj5mMBg.

"You Waited," Travis Scott, https://music.youtube.com/watch?v=-cyzbge2QEF4&list=RDAMVMcyzbge2QEF4.

"You Made a Way," Travis Scott, https://music.youtube.com/ watch?v=MimVg0OMGvA&list=RDAMVMOP-00EwLdiU.

"You Deserve It," JJ Hairson, https://music.youtube.com/watch?v=GjPehgvSLH0&list=OLAK5uy_kcAvrsgQxr2YjF1xOd-2rhy-DC3Sx0B8c2U.

"The Anthem," William Murphy, https://music.youtube.com/ watch?v=Arux7US8WZ0.

"Fill Me Up," Casey J, https://music.youtube.com/watch?v=Inywc7hW14s.

"Jehovah Jireh," Maverick City, https://music.youtube.com/ watch?v=mC-zw0zCCtg&list=RDAMVMOP-00EwLdiU.

"Oceans," Hillsong, https://music.youtube.com/watch?v=OP-00EwLdiU&list=RDAMVMOP-00EwLdiU.

"Reckless Love," Corey Asbury, https://music.youtube.com/ watch?v=6xx0d3R2LoU&list=RDAMVMOP-00EwLdiU.

"You Say," Lauren Daigle, https://music.youtube.com/watch?v=sI-aT8Jl2zpI&list=RDAMVMOP-00EwLdiU.

"Order in My Steps," Choir, https://music.youtube.com/watch?v=Inywc7hW14s.

Meditation

Let's slow it down a little.

"I'll Just Say Yes," Brian Courtney Wilson, https://music.youtube.com/watch?v=Nh45V2ODGyA.

"Mention," Fresh Start Worship, https://music.youtube.com/ watch?v=YVROt32teYo.

"God Will Make a Way," Angel911, https://music.youtube.com/watch?v=1zo3fJYtS-o.

"What a Beautiful Name It Is," Hillsong, https://music.youtube.com/watch?v=Yh3GtsFP8NM.

"Open My Heart," Yolanda Adams, https://music.youtube.com/ watch?v=8p4sMV_N6jQ.

"Your Spirit," Tasha Cobbs, https://music.youtube.com/watch?v=B-ZT8jqsc8lQ.

"Yunka Okeleye," Worship, https://music.youtube.com/ watch?v=aAHs98Vm_jI.

"Everlasting God," William Murphy, https://music.youtube.com/ watch?v=TMKzffVKY3s.

"Forever," Jason Nelson, https://music.youtube.com/watch?v=FnVFe_J2zfI.

Christian Rap

"Tell the World," Lecrae, https://music.youtube.com/watch?v=uY1MRnoOrEM.

"Sweet Victory," Trip Lee https://music.youtube.com/watch?v=ptG-MjBenTdM&list=RDAMVMuY1MRnoOrEM.

"You Can't Stop Me," Andy Mineo, https://music.youtube.com/ watch?v=2Wf50NDBYK4.

"Oh Lord," NF, https://music.youtube.com/watch?v=W-xAW4nj-WEI.

"Home," Tedashi, https://music.youtube.com/watch?v=wgCGejH-gW2I.

"God Over Money," Bizzle, https://music.youtube.com/watch?v=zc-M58VCpDsg&list=RDAMVMZBshbsz1nGg.

DO YOU KNOW ME OR JUST THE NAME?

"God on my Side," Social Misfits, https://music.youtube.com/ watch ?v=i2mcoh-IAiM.

"Jesus Freak," DC Talk, https://music.youtube.com/ watch?v=8hy U5Z7z0D8.

"Church Clap," KB, https://music.youtube.com/watch?v=mzGElp-TUcWs.

"God Taught Me," Zauntee, https://music.youtube.com/watch?v=X-ONeznR30Sk&list=RDAMVMZBshbsz1nGg.

"Grateful," - 1Pkhew, https://music.youtube.com/watch?v=D0BUF t2ZVrE&list=OLAK5uy_kZTo_HV9-0uUADui40Gu6Cfk-gYTueBs4Y.

So many more.

Old-School Gospel Singers

Old Time Gospel Quartet: https://music.youtube.com/watch?v=tYs-1moZi7VI&list=OLAK5uy_ktBeGz4rogRLxAd6JzcTFNsk-M6qMEn_Io.

Golden Gospel Singers: https://music.youtube.com/watch?v=kHxECp 4U_DA.

Jim Reeves: https://music.youtube.com/watch?v=hhxolymJ11Q& list=PL7q46xJd_TS4ULWvpUjUJGs7S2bqxfhwG.

Mississippi Mass Choir: https://music.youtube.com/watch?v=G-Pwp-jg6mHc&list=OLAK5uy_mOUgZfMviWMebvn4tPc-c9Wp2IA3OiA-64.

Let's Dance

"Give Me," Kirk Franklin, https://music.youtube.com/watch?v= bR6a5SWVRoo.

"In the Middle," Isaac Carree, https://music.youtube.com/watch?v= uxtdql1Crsc.

"War," Charles Jenkins, https://music.youtube.com/watch?v=LrIoG-g3TL-A.

Reference Bible Teachers

Dr. Tony Evans
Kay Arthur
David Jerimiah
Charles Stanley
Priscilla Shirer

There are so many more.

About the Author

Janet, who is the mother of four children, sets goals for herself. She is also a Sunday-school, life group leader for over five years with missionary and voluntary experience.

Printed in the USA
CPSIA information can be obtained
at www.ICGtesting.com
CBHW050342180724
11672CB00026B/577